The Magic of High-Quality Questions

The Magic of High-Quality Questions

A Recipe for Success in Business, in Relationships, in Life

Robert Shemin and Hugh O. Stewart

iUniverse, Inc.
Bloomington

The Magic of High-Quality Questions
A Recipe for Success in Business, in Relationships, in Life

iUniverse books may be ordered through booksellers or by contacting:

iUniverse
1663 Liberty Drive
Bloomington, IN 47403
www.iuniverse.com
1-800-Authors (1-800-288-4677)

ISBN: 978-1-4620-2831-3 (pbk)
ISBN: 978-1-4620-2832-0 (ebk)

Library of Congress Control Number: 2011909655

Printed in the United States of America

iUniverse rev. date: 06/22/2011

Contents

Introduction

Dead-End Dialogue

Good communication skills are, without question, vital for anyone in any field in order to be successful. In learning about communication, we are taught how to speak well, how to formulate and organize thoughts, how to implement good body language, and we're even taught how to listen well. What I find missing in this arena is question-asking skills. I find that little thought or preparation goes into how questions are used to create the best results.

Because of this, there is a great deal of dead-end dialogue going on that passes for conversation. It often goes nowhere, and often brings about the total opposite result from what was originally intended.

Why? Because the actual *intention* was never scrutinized or examined. One of the things I have been personally passionate about is recognizing the intention behind the questions being asked, because the intention can make the difference between being a millionaire or being broke and out on the street. Yes, it's *that* crucial.

High-Quality Questions

It's interesting that people invest a great amount of time in study to prepare for a career, or in training for an athletic event, or in setting up a business deal, or starting a business. But how much time is spent in preparing to ask high-quality questions that make our lives function on a higher level?

Every facet of our lives thrives on workable solutions and yet we spend little time considering the setup, or the nature, of the questions we ask.

One of the goals for this book, is to have people recognize that in many instances the very nature of their ability to succeed or get what they want in this world, is absolutely dependent on the quality of certain questions.

You may be wondering how the simple act of asking high-quality questions could make that much difference. I invite you to come along and discover for yourself.

Meet the Characters

In this book, you will meet two divergent personalities who, upon a chance meeting in the park one day, become close friends. They are a generation apart. Sol, known as *Sol the Sage* by his close friends, has been around the block a few times. His passion is imparting wisdom to the up and coming generation. Which is not always that easy since so few care to listen and learn.

Ron, known as *Ron the Rookie,* to Sol only, is young and somewhat overly confident. Jogging through the park early each morning before his commute to his corporate job in the city, he barely sees the older man on the park bench.

Following their initial meeting and subsequent meetings, Ron is set up to learn a great deal about question-asking skills from The Sage. And as a result, things in his life change for the better in ways he never thought possible.

By using the concepts and principles that Sol introduces in the pages of this book, you can experience changes in your life as well.

To Your Success
Robert and Hugh

[NOTE: Although the pronoun "I" is used in this introduction, the premises and concepts presented here are shared equally by both authors.]

Chapter 1

A Chance Meeting

Sol leaned his gray head back against the park bench and closed his eyes against the early morning autumn sun that bathed his face. Another gorgeous day was in the making. The trees were brilliant with color, and yet it was nearly as warm as a Spring day.

There were a number of the regulars out jogging the footpaths. Sol himself had already run a few miles, before the sun came up. One young fellow never failed to capture Sol's attention. Fit and lean, he was always in a tug-of-war with a full-grown boxer he called Gretchen. Sol often chuckled watching them, wondering who was walking whom. Gretchen had a mind of her own.

As usual, right on time, the young jogger came down the track that led around the lake. Sol could hear him calling out to the dog. The lines were always the same. Sol could recite them by heart.

"Gretchen, what's wrong with you?"

"Gretchen, why can't you mind me?"

"Gretchen, why in the world did I ever pay for obedience school for you?"

"Gretchen, why do you always go off that direction? You know we never go that way."

Sol watched and smiled.

On Saturdays, the scene shifted somewhat. Instead of running with the dog, a little boy was in tow—along with the dog. On these mornings the father slowed his pace to accommodate the boy. Now his questions were addressed to the son, who looked to be about seven or eight. But they were similar to the questions he asked the dog!

"Michael, what's wrong with you?"

"Michael, why can't you mind me?"

"Michael, why are you going toward the lake? You know we never go that way."

"Michael, come on! Do you want to be late for soccer practice?"

Intention Behind the Questions

One particular Saturday morning Sol was walking the path when he spotted Ron coming toward him with the dog on a leash and son Michael trotting out ahead. Just as they approached, the boy spotted a toad hopping through the grass. "Look, a toad!" he yelled, and shot out after it. In doing so, he crossed the path and ran smack into Sol.

Sol, laughing, caught the boy just before he fell.

Michael's attention, however, was still on the fat toad in the grass.

"Michael," his father said, "what were you thinking? Why don't you watch where you're going?" Then looking at Sol, he said somewhat curtly, "Sorry. He never watches where he's going."

Sol released the boy's shoulders, who then continued the toad chase. Looking intently at the young *rookie,* Sol said, "So, tell me, young man, how did you intend for Michael to answer your questions?"

"What? What're you talking about? Michael, get back over here. We're late now."

"The questions . . ."

"Yeah I heard you. What questions? I don't know what you're talking about."

"You asked your son two questions."

"Two?"

"Yes. Two questions. 'What were you thinking?' and 'Why don't you watch where you're going?' I was curious as to how you intended for him to answer."

Ron scowled. "What are you, nuts? Come on Michael. Leave that thing alone."

By now Michael had caught the toad, but his father insisted he let it go and they hurried on their way.

Sol watched them go, smiling and shaking his head.

Pay Close Attention to the Questions

A few days went by before Sol saw the young jogger again. As usual Sol was resting on his favorite park bench watching the ducks skimming the pond. He hadn't really noticed until the figure was standing almost right in front of him.

The young man stepped right up and thrust out his hand. "I'm Ron," he said.

Sol returned the handshake. "They call me Sol the Sage."

Ron stood there a moment. "I may not be the sharpest tool in the toolbox, but I think you were trying to tell me something the other day. I can't get it out of my mind. Something about questions."

"A very important subject—questions. Had you ever thought about questions before?"

"Can't say as I have. Look, I've got to get downtown and I don't have much time. Can you give me the condensed version?"

"Sure." Sol smiled and his eyes twinkled. "You youngsters are always in such a hurry." Sol motioned to the bench and Ron sat down beside him. "The condensed version is this. You asked your son questions. Did you think about your intentions when asking them? Did you think about what he could do next after the questions were presented?"

A blank stare registered on Ron's face. "I didn't think about any of that. Was I supposed to?"

"What's your line of work, Ron?"

"I'm the sales manager in a manufacturing company."

"Hmm. I would think that position would lend itself to asking many question all throughout the day."

Ron thought about that. "You're right. It does."

"Well, then, you might want to pay closer attention to the questions you ask and how you ask them." Sol could tell this rookie still wasn't quite grasping it.

Ron stood to his feet. "I've got to go now. But I want to hear more. Maybe we could meet over a cup of coffee sometime. Here's my number." He was scribbling on a piece of paper pulled from his wind breaker pocket.

Sol nodded. "I'd like that. I'll give you a call."

As Ron jogged away, Sol heaved a sigh. "Ah," he whispered to himself. "An open heart; an open mind."

What's the Big Deal?

Ron was surprised when a message from Sol registered on his cell phone. Sol suggested they meet at the park earlier than usual the next morning, jog together, then spend a few minutes chatting at the coffee shop across from the park.

So the old Sage jogs? This is getting more interesting, Ron thought. At their first meeting, Ron had to admit he thought the old geezer was nuts. But now his curiosity was piqued. Since he was used to slowing his pace for his son, he could do the same for old Sol. Ron agreed to the plan. He decided Gretchen could sit this one out.

It was still dark when the two joined up to jog twice around the lake. All thoughts of slowing down were cast aside; it was all Ron could do to keep up with his new friend. It was spitting rain when they entered the coffee shop and placed their order. Ron was still breathing heavy. He tried to veil his surprise at Sol's prowess by putting on his nonchalant pose he often used at work.

"So what's all this stuff about asking questions? I've run this over in my mind, but I can't see your point. What's the big deal about how you ask a question?"

Sol raised his shaggy eyebrows as he sipped from his steaming cup. "I'm so glad you asked," he said. "For this morning, I'm going to give you the bare-bones basics. Then if you want to explore the subject even deeper, we'll make time meet again. Agreed?"

Ron nodded. "Agreed."

Chapter 2

The Bare-Bones Basics of Asking High-Quality Questions

Take the Time to Plan

To grasp a fuller understanding of the basics of asking high-quality questions, one must back up and look at the *purposes* for asking. There are two objectives which can govern the nature of nearly every question.

- ***The first is to protect and deepen your confidence and the confidence of those to whom you are speaking.***
- ***The second is to inspire the imagination. Because when you inspire the imagination, the ability to do the impossible becomes possible.***

The catalyst behind these two purposes is intention. What was the core intention behind asking the questions in the first place? In order to know this, one must stop and take the time to plan.

Let's take a vivid illustration of this point. French high wire artist, Philippe Petit, did the impossible on August 7, 1974. With help from a few friends, he strung a high wire between the two World Trade Center towers and proceeded to walk across. This artist, who knew his profession well, did not hurry. He did not rush. In fact, his *performance* lasted nearly one hour. He was literally dangling out in space with nothing below to stop a fall, but he did not hurry.

The point is that the same principle applies to life—to living. Most people don't realize that as they walk through their day, as they interact with other people, they are walking a virtual tight rope. If you rush through your day there is a chance that you might fall off and you don't even know.

Those who say, "I'm busy, I don't have time," are saying, "I am rushing on the tight rope. It's okay to rush on the tight rope, and it's okay to live my life not paying attention to what I say or how I frame my questions to others."

The Need to be Right

The matter of framing high-quality questions then is about awareness to the world around you. It's an awareness of how you are feeling about your range of expectation for yourself and others. It's a mechanism for you to appreciate awareness; to become aware of how you are interacting with your world, your surroundings, the people who make things happen, and ultimately an awareness of yourself as well. The point here is to take a millisecond to orient yourself to the appropriate intention behind the questions you ask.

It's probably safe to say that 98.9% of questions that are asked are for people to confirm their own preconditioned, predetermined, limited ideas. This is because everyone wants to *feel better and feel right.* Their intention is not to get a real answer, or see how the other person is really feeling, or really thinking, or to learn what's really going on in a particular situation. Consciously or subconsciously, the person asking the question is thinking: "I've got an idea and I am going to ask that question to demonstrate that I'm right."

The need to be right closes so many doors. It's as though you close yourself off from the world. When you must be right, you are usually not closely connected with others around you. You are isolated on an island alone, enjoying your rightness.

You can walk past someone at your workplace. "How are you?" you ask quickly. The answer comes back, "Doing great."

Chances are, later on you won't remember that conversation. There is no intention behind the question. This is opposed to taking one second, taking a breath, and just thinking about your intention.

I want to brighten up this person's day. I want to take a quick moment and really make a connection and see how my friend, or co-worker, or family member is doing. So I stop and ask a pointed question to show a true interest in that person's life and their well being. It all comes back to intention. If you want to operate under the right intention, stop for a moment and get yourself out of your automatic, hypnotic, auto-pilot-type of questioning style. Take a breath and then instead of asking a thoughtless question with no clear intention, ask a high-quality question.

An Approach Comparison

Ron listened intently as Sol walked him through these basic points, nodding often. "I've experienced exactly what you're talking about," Ron said, after which he relayed this story.

> *After I graduated from graduate school, I took a job in San Jose, Costa Rica. I spoke fluent Spanish and I went to work at a busy international organization. I was amazed that when I walked down the hallway, my co-workers—if I knew them even slightly—would stop and say,* "Hola, coma estas?" *Hello, how are you doing? More than likely that co-worker would give me a hug or kiss me on the cheek. They would actually stop and make eye contact. After asking "how are you?" they would stop.*
>
> *The first couple of times it happened, I would pause and say, "What do you want?" But I quickly learned that they were truly interested in my answer.*
>
> *These people actually stopped and made a connection. They asked and then they stopped—they were waiting for a real answer.*

> *If I answered,* "I'm okay, how are you?" *They might talk about their family or their kids or how work was going. At first this exchange was almost annoying. I'm an American, after all.*
>
> *It didn't take long before I came to enjoy it. It became touching to me that these people stopped, asked a question, and cared about the answer. It would be viewed as rude or unacceptable if you didn't take just a moment to make that connection.*
>
> *When I left San Jose, Costa Rica, I took a job in Manhattan on Wall Street. This is a place where everyone is in a rush. I remember literally sprinting down the hallway and people shouting out, "Hey, how're you doing?" And I would shout back, "Great! How're you doing?" I didn't stop, and no one expected me to. I had innumerable tasks to get done and had little time.*
>
> *I'm not saying one culture is right and another is wrong, but I am saying that having lived those two contrasting experiences I am beginning to see what you're getting at.*

Sol helped Ron to see that it's not a matter of right or wrong, but of learning from each situation. Shouting out a question greeting has precious little intention, and even less expectation behind it; therefore it accomplishes little. This takes us back to the two objectives behind the formulation of our questions.

- ***The first is to protect and deepen your confidence and the confidence of those to whom you are speaking.***
- ***The second is to inspire the imagination. Because when you inspire the imagination, the ability to do the impossible becomes possible.***

A quick "How're you doing?" fails with both.

At the close of their talk, Ron was wavering between a glimmer of understanding and a loss as how to implement much of what he'd learned.

Sol was not perturbed in the least, but simply suggested they set up a once-a-week meeting to dig deeper into the subject of asking high-quality questions.

Ron agreed that it might take several sessions for him to fully grasp these concepts. "But I'm willing to start practicing what I've already learned."

"Great," Sol said pushing back his chair to go. "Just a word of warning."

"What's that?"

"This may not work with Gretchen!"

Chapter 3

Digging Deeper

Will That Solve the Problem?

There was more of a chill in the air the next time the two men jogged together. Ron wasn't thinking about slowing down this morning. Now he knew what to expect, and put his pace into full form. This time, Gretchen came along. Ron insisted she'd lie quietly when they talked at the coffee shop. The warmth of the coffee shop was a welcome respite after their run in the cold air.

"I've been paying close attention this past week, not only to how I ask questions, but how others ask them as well," Ron said as they waited for the hot coffee and toasted bagels to be served.

"Did you come to any conclusions?" Sol wanted to know.

Ron shook his head. "Not much."

"Want to work on few specifics?"

"That's easy. I have this salesman who drives me nuts. He'll do fine for a month or so, then he starts coming in late and not keeping up with quotas. He's full of excuses. I've tried everything I know, but I can't seem to get the problem solved."

"Tell me exactly what it is that you've *tried.*"

"I'm very firm with him and demand to know why he's late!"

"So you're asking this salesman why he's late, is that correct?"

"Exactly."

"Is that what you really want to know? Are you that interested in *why* he's late? Is it your mission to know why he's late? Will that answer or solve the problem?"

Range of Possibilities

Ron stared out the window for a moment watching the cold wind rip the last of the leaves off the trees in the park. "I guess I thought it would, but all I ever hear are more excuses. Or he just ducks his head and says he'll try to do better."

"Think about your intention when you ask the question, *Why were you late?* What is your state of mind when you ask?"

"I'm angry; I'm frustrated; I'm fed up and I want him to know it." Ron had to laugh. "I guess that puts him on the defensive doesn't it?"

"It does," Sol answered, "and if your intention is to make him feel bad, or remorseful, then you are disempowering that individual."

"I never thought of it like that. *Disempower.* That isn't moving toward a good solution."

"You admit you are in a state of agitation. When you ask a question in a state of being upset, your question is sure to reflect that. In other words, you're using the question to let that person *know* you are upset."

"You're right. I *do* want him to know I'm upset."

"Yet the problem is still goes unresolved, and now you have an employee who even if he has the best excuse in the world for being late, is being demeaned by the accusatory question."

Ron considered this. He could see the wisdom in the point Sol made, but still saw no alternative. Being the tough boss is how he had built his sales team to where it was. He prided himself on not taking any guff from anyone. "So, what would you do?"

Sol smiled. "I'm not the sales manager, remember? It's your team you're building. Just think about this particular sales person for a moment. There has to be a modicum of success for this individual to even be with your company—or to be on your team. Is that correct?"

"I only hire the best," Ron bragged.

"Consider then how you can honor this person's past successes, honor his assets and be careful not to ignore what value brought him to this point." Sol paused for a moment while the waitperson refilled his coffee cup, then he went on. "And then consider the range of possibilities open to this person. After being asked an accusatory question, asked while you're upset, what action steps can this salesman take next?"

Ron leaned back in his chair. The light was beginning to dawn—not only outside, but on Ron's face. "I've totally shut down his range of possibilities."

"Wise observation," Sol said.

Questions on Automatic Pilot

It doesn't take a great deal of scrutiny to realize that most of the questions that we put forth on a daily basis are on automatic pilot with very little thought or planning. People are in a non-conscious, almost hypnotic state where most of the questions are pre-programmed in the person's mind. We could call these *low-quality questions.*

At first glance this may seem a small matter. However, the majority of people's problems, whether it be in relationships, business, money, health or whatever, come from asking these ineffective low-quality questions.

Such questions are usually structured so that it limits the ability to move forward. For instance, "*why*" questions limit creativity. When Ron asked the employee, "Why were you late?" the subsequent actions were limited.

You may want them to reflect on their actions, but you don't want to prevent them from taking the next step. If they have to answer the *why* question, it takes longer to get to your desired outcome. So save time and ask the efficient, high-quality questions.

Ask the Efficient, High-Quality Questions

Here's an example:

> *"I see that you were late today and that is unacceptable behavior. What do we have to do to make sure you come to work on time without fail?"*

You've addressed the problem. You made it clear that the actions are unacceptable. The question then opens the way for creativity and possibility thinking. Let's make it even more efficient:

> *"I know that you have an incredible amount of potential in you, but there seems to be something standing in the way. I noticed that you were very late to work today and that is not acceptable behavior. What do we have to do to make sure that you achieve your potential by coming to work on time every single day? What can I do to support that activity and what do you need to start changing to make sure that you are here to show up for your success?"*

It's good to ask yourself how a question makes you *feel*. Does the question make you feel disempowered, agitated, confused? Or does it make you feel energized and filled with confidence and endless possibilities? Ron had to confess that his sales staff members were probably often agitated and confused by his questions.

Two Questions; Two Responses

Sol then shared an experience that shed more light on this aspect of asking the most efficient questions.

> *When I was doing my first real estate investment deal, I basically did everything wrong that a person could possibly do in buying a house. I was fairly young at*

the time. The house was near where I lived and I often admired the well-kept yard.

One day it went up for sale. Being curious, I went up and knocked on the door. I said I noticed the for sale sign in the yard to which they answered that they were just renting the place. They were an elderly couple and I was surprised that they were renters simply because of how well they kept the place.

Inwardly I knew I just had to buy that house. Not knowing what I was doing, I told them that if I bought the house, I would let them stay and keep their rent the same. (That was my first mistake.)

I then contracted to pay way too much for the house, but I was a green investor and I was ecstatic. The mortgage company told me that I would be able to get any number of loans put together for 95% financing for the house. That didn't happen. Basically, everything fell apart. The mortgage broker got back to me—three weeks after we were supposed to close—and informed me that I only qualified for 65% financing.

That meant I had to find over $38,000 in order to close in 48-72 hours and get this deal. I remember sitting down at my desk and writing two questions on a sheet of paper. The first question asked "What am I doing?"

The second question asked, "How am I going to find $38,000 in 72 hours?"

When I looked at the first question I felt panic and concern; I felt stress and worry.

When I contemplated the second question I felt possibility surging up inside me. So much so that I was ready to max out all my credit cards if I had to, or go to my parents for help, whatever it took I was willing to do it. At that moment an enormous amount of creativity overtook me and from that moment I only contemplated the possibility of answering the second question.

> *I went to lunch that day at a Chinese buffet restaurant. When I opened the fortune cookie at the end of the meal, the message inside read:* "Unlimited opportunities await you after this very crucial step."
>
> *From that point I got focused and I went ahead and bought the house. Would I do that deal today knowing what I know? Absolutely not! But at the time it was very important for me to move forward.*

The point here is that two different questions brought forth two completely opposite responses. So even in self-talk, asking high-quality questions is crucial. It's important to take a moment and gauge the response that a question brings forth.

* * *

As the two men stood up to leave, Ron stopped for a moment. Sol could tell there was something else on his mind.

"I guess in the park the other morning when I asked Michael 'What were you thinking?' I didn't leave him much in the range of possibilities, did I?"

Sol shook his head. "Nor did it instill confidence."

As Ron went out the door he knew he had a lot to think about. He also knew that he was ready to put these concepts into action in his sales department starting that very day.

As Sol the Sage turned to walk home, he was humming a little tune to himself. It was such a pleasure to discover a rookie who was willing to learn.

Chapter 4

Four Levels of Communication

Changing the Question Opened the Door

Sol and Ron sat enjoying chilled bottles of Gatorade after a strenuous bout of racquetball. It was Ron's idea to meet at his gym for this session together. Ron had beat out his older opponent in the game—but just barely. Each time they met, Sol the Sage was earning more of the Rookie's respect.

As they sat there catching their breath, Ron took the opportunity to share some of his successes the past week.

It seems the salesman who was continually late, had a valid reason after all. "This salesman, Jason, has a ten-year-old daughter with a heart condition," Ron said, wiping sweat off his face with the towel draped around his neck. "The girl is homebound for a few weeks, and it seems the caregiver, or the school tutor, seem to show up just as he is ready to leave for work."

"And no one at the office knew about this?"

Ron shook his head. "Maybe his closest associates knew, but I sure didn't. So when I asked the question like you suggested—"*What do we have to do to make sure that you achieve your potential by coming to work on time every single day?*—Jason teared up and then told me the story."

"Changing the form of question opened the door," Sol put in.

"It did," Ron agreed.

"What happened next?"

"We sat down and worked out a different time schedule for him." Ron smiled. "It's already working. And get this. Jason said the reason he had not told me before was that he didn't want to appear as though he were looking for pity. He said he wanted to stay on an even keel with his peers."

"I'm pleased for you, Ron. That's a big step in the right direction."

"But that's not all. I've begun to stop and think more often before I speak. I'm putting thought and planning into the questions I ask."

"And the results?"

Ron took a long drink of Gatorade before answering. "I seem to be more relaxed and more confident." He shook his head. "It's difficult to pin down or describe." Then he looked at Sol and smiled. "But I like it better than the old way."

Questions Can Limit Possibilities

Sol understood perfectly, in spite of the fact that Ron was having difficulty putting into words what had happened. Essentially Ron had transformed an investigative question, "Why are you late?" into an empowering question that made it possible for his staff member to take an action step. Additionally, the empowering question (*What do we have to do to make sure that you achieve your potential by coming to work on time every single day?*) drew the two of them into a partnership of resolving the issue. Ron quickly learned that his subordinate, Jason, was eager to adjust his schedule and get his sales quotas back up where they'd been before.

For the most part, *why* questions (because of the way they are often asked) already assume a defensive position and a limited range of possibility. Demanding, investigative, *why* questions are often rooted in negativity; and negativity is often rooted in fear.

Sol talked to Ron about the four levels of communication. "The problem with the demanding, investigative question," he said, "is that it's a very surface level type of communication. A communication that doesn't care much about the response."

Here are the four types of communication as Sol described them:

Level 1: The first level of communication is what we call "small talk." *How are you? I'm fine. That's good.* It happens every day in all walks of life and in all cultures. It is not without purpose, because it's often used as an ice breaker to get to the next level.

Level 2: The second level goes a little deeper, but is mostly factual such as:

My major is in computer sciences.
I'm a single mom with two children, a son and a daughter.
Do you root for the Dallas Cowboys?
What was the assignment the professor gave last Wednesday?

This level can be somewhat superficial as the answers may be phrased to make the individual appear more intellectual, or more important, or more secure than he or she truly is.

Level 3: The third level of communication can be more on the evaluative approach. Opinions can be stated—but usually very carefully. You might want to say that your deepest dream is to be on a beach in the Caribbean writing poetry, but you're fearful of the response that statement might bring. People might think you're crazy.

On this level, giving heartfelt opinions and ideas mean that another's opinions and ideas will be offered as well. This is where conflict can arise; and if there is no mutual respect this is also where dreams can be destroyed.

Level 4: The fourth level delves deeper into the innermost heart of personal dreams and aspirations. As with level three, this can be a risky area, and will only be reached after trust is built and fear has been overcome. On this level you will learn more about the *real* person with the defenses down. On this level you yourself will be more vulnerable as well.

On level four, you might ask a subordinate at the workplace:

"What about your work here is the most fulfilling to you?"

"Where do you see yourself going in the company? What are your highest aspirations?"

"What can I do to assist you in reaching your goals?"

A Startling Discovery

As Ron thought about the communication levels, and as he thought about Sol's statement about fear, he came to a startling discovery. He realized that, basically, he had been interacting with his subordinates through a degree of fear.

"I realized from the outset," he confessed to Sol, "that this sales team had the power to make or break me. They could make me look good to those above me, or make me look like a loser. That's a scary thought."

From that point Sol was able to help Ron determine from where he sourced his value. A person's value can be sourced from those around you, or it can come from within. If it comes from within, you then know that you are confident enough to overcome the fear. In fact, that sums up Sol's definition of confidence.

Confidence is the capability to transform fear into very specific thinking and action using your best skills with your best resources.

You can source value wherever you want; however, recognizing that you are valuable allows you to believe that you have the ability to be creative. Creative enough to ask the questions that allow you to unleash the unlimited potential that exists within you. And also to ask questions to unleash unlimited potential that exists within others around you. You can believe that you are *enough.* If you are able to metabolize fear to the degree that the more fear there is surrounding you, the more confidence you are able to generate for yourself. Thus you become afraid of no one.

The Power of One Question

To drive this point home, Sol shared the true story of an acquaintance of his named Robert, who struggled through childhood with dyslexia. This was before the condition was as well known as it is today. Here is Robert's story.

> *Growing up I had a very rare form of dyslexia that was not diagnosed correctly until I was eighteen years old. As a result, I did poorly in school. I was bored all the time. The question that I heard over and over again—from teachers, guidance counselors, family members and friends—was* "What's wrong with you?"
>
> *It was obvious I wasn't dumb. I had a high degree of intelligence, but I made poor grades and I was always bored. I began to act out in school and continually got into trouble.*
>
> *Now I surmised that most of these people were pretty smart, so they must be right. Those teachers, the principal, the guidance counselors must know* something, *I told myself, so they must be right. There must be something* really *wrong with me! Consequently I began the same self talk:* "I wonder what's wrong with me?"
>
> *Then I would come home from school and all of my family members asked the same thing.* "You're getting bad grades; you're not doing well in school; you're getting in trouble! Why? What's wrong with you?"
>
> *So, I focused on that question a great deal as a kid growing up. However, there was one person who never asked me that question. That was my grandmother, whom we called Nanny.*
>
> *Nanny always put forth a positive outlook no matter what was going on in her children's or grandchildren's lives. Her family was the total focus of her existence. She loved to take care of us, cook for us, and make us happy.*

No matter what my cousins or my siblings were doing, she was always positive about everything.

Nanny never asked me, "What's wrong with you?" *She never asked,* "What's your problem?" *or* "Why aren't you doing better in school?"

One day as we were sitting around our big dining room table during a family dinner, I was being interrogated once again. I'd gotten into trouble and had been expelled from school. And again the barrage came forth: "What's wrong with you?" "You're never going to amount to anything." "You'll probably never graduate from high school."

Nanny, on the other hand, was unaffected. None of what they said swayed her. Out of her confidence she looked across the table and said, "Robert, you're so personable and you're such a wonderful guy. You're good looking and everybody likes you."

All of the sudden I started feeling fantastic.

Then she asked me a question. "Robert, what would you really, really like to do with your school life?"

At that moment I felt positive and happy. I'd already thought about this a great deal but had never told a soul. I said, "I would like to go to college."

The words had barely left my lips when my family members started smirking and laughing. After all, it's pretty hard to get into college with a 0.01 high school grade average.

But Nanny still had eye contact with me, and she wasn't laughing at me. So I continued as though she were the only person in the room. "I want to own my own business someday. But I would really like to continue my studies and get a joint law and business degree." *Nanny was beaming with joy at my answers as the other fourteen people at the table howled with laughter.*

Suddenly their laughter meant nothing. I paid no attention. I focused on Nanny's smiling face. Just speaking those words aloud made all the difference.

I did almost flunk out of high school, but I got accepted to a college. Once I discovered I had dyslexia, I learned how to deal with it and how to rise above it. I became serious and focused, and made straight A's the very first semester.

I later transferred to Vanderbilt University, one of the best in the country. I went on to receive a joint Law and MBA Degree from Emory University.

I often think about Nanny and her courageous question. I later realized that it wasn't only what she asked but how she asked it.

I was accustomed to people asking me questions with a mean vindictive demeanor in their voice and body language which actually said: "You're an idiot." "You're stupid." "You're dumb." *Not with Nanny. She asked me questions as though I were the most intelligent, smartest, greatest person on earth. When she looked at me I knew she was sincerely interested in the real answer. She made me believe I was capable of accomplishing anything I set my mind to!*

Begin at Home

After hearing this captivating story, Ron had to agree that this grandmother was communicating to her grandson on the deeper Fourth Level of communication. The questions she asked were high-quality questions. She touched a chord that no one else seemed to have touched—or bothered to touch. And it changed the young man's life.

Ron's thoughts turned toward his wife and son, the two people he was closer to than anyone else in the world. He resolved to begin to communicate with both of them on a deeper level than ever before. And he would do it by asking caring, intentional questions.

Chapter 5

Creativity

Yes or No Questions

At a small restaurant near Ron's downtown office, Ron and Sol were talking over lunch. Ron had asked Sol to come and visit his office and meet a few of the employees. Sol derived great pleasure in seeing Ron interacting with his sales personnel. It was clear that he was well respected. The fact that sales were up—well, Ron just said it had something to do with asking questions.

They had spent the morning together and were now capping it off with time to once again discuss the subject (which Ron now found totally intriguing) of asking high-quality questions.

Today, Sol was discussing creativity—a topic near to his heart. "It grieves me to hear people asking questions that shut down creativity," he was saying as they waited for their sandwiches to be served.

"Such as?"

"There are a number of offenders, but one that is near the top of the list is a question that can be answered by yes or no."

Ron sprinkled a packet of sweetener into his coffee and stirred thoughtfully. "I guess I'm an offender in that category," he said. "I ask a lot of questions to which the answers would be yes or no. What's the problem with that?"

"Basically, anything that allows you to answer a question in a yes or no framework destroys creativity—categorically. Think about it this way.

A yes answer, if it's affirmative, is solutions-based and you stop thinking. A negative answer will put you on the defensive, which also shuts down creative thinking. So whether you answer yes, or you answer no, you have completely bypassed the creative process. It does little or nothing to foster creative thoughts and ideas."

"Can you give an example?" Ron asked.

"Sure. Let's say you want to move forward with a new business idea. And you ask your spouse, 'Can we afford to do this?' What's the answer to that question?"

Ron chuckled. "It has to be a yes or a no."

"And will that line of questioning move any closer to launching a new business? Or even considering a plan for a new business?"

"Nowhere near," Ron agreed. "It would be better to present the idea for the new business, and then ask 'How do you think we can make this happen?' And then ask for ideas and input."

"Now you're getting the picture." Sol said, and took a big bite out of his Reuben sandwich.

Is it Worth It?

"What's another example of a question that shuts down creativity?"

"One that I hear a lot: 'Is it worth it?' This can quickly sabotage any action plan."

Ron looked puzzled. "Okay, now give an example for that one."

"Say, it's the beginning of a new year. An individual knows he needs to get on an exercise program. He's been thinking it about it, but it always comes down to asking himself, 'Is it really worth it?'"

Ron's face lit up immediately. "Oh, I see. So then he begins to list all the reasons why it might not be worth it, right?"

"You got it."

"People do that in a lot of areas, don't they? Taking the example we used earlier, an individual is considering starting a new business, but he continually asks himself, 'Is it worth it?'"

Sol nodded. "And immediately creativity is completely shut down. There is no space for solution thinking. Instead, what if the question were: "How can I make going into this business the most profitable decision I have ever made?'"

"Whoa!" Ron almost knocked over his water glass as he waved his arm in excitement. "Now that's a solution-seeking question if I ever heard one."

"And empowering?"

"And empowering," Ron agreed.

Be Quiet and Ingest the Question

As the two men talked that day through Ron's extended lunch hour, Sol had a number of illustrations of how simply changing a question, or thoroughly thinking through a question, opens the door to limitless creativity—which in turn leads to workable solutions.

He pointed out how important it is to have a goal in mind about what you want to accomplish with the question being asked. But where the magic happens in fostering creativity is in the silence right after the question is asked. This is the moment when you almost *ingest* the question. Before you even think about an answer, just contemplate for a moment. This can be called contemplation, or even meditation.

Sol confessed that many ideas and solutions that he felt were truly creative in his life came from places that "I had no idea I had any connection to." That gap between the question and the solution is where your fire of creativity really emanates. You access that by asking the right questions and getting quiet for a moment.

You may have a couple of thoughts that may provide solutions, but that's not really where the power is. The power is in the contemplation and the gestation right after the question is asked—bringing it into yourself, and allowing the unconditioned self inside of you to start working on the solution. You actually believe for a second that the answer will feel good, and then it comes. And it may be something that you had no idea about.

Focus on the Problem; Or Focus on the Solution

Of all the stories that Sol shared that day regarding creativity, this one was Ron's favorite.

> *In one of the businesses that I owned, I was faced with a problem regarding hiring. For some reason, I didn't have enough qualified applicants for a particular chain of stores. I spoke with the operations manager and she told me that she was concerned that we would probably have to lower our standards for the quality of candidates coming in to our system.*
>
> *I seem to remember the question that she asked was,* "Do we need to lower our standards?"
>
> *That question revealed to me now only how discouraged she felt, but also her limited range of expectation, and range of possibility. The only thing she could contemplate at the moment was to lower the bar.*
>
> *But I thought there should be more options. So, I took a second and assessed the situation. First of all, I believed there must be an abundance of people who wanted to work for a great company like mine. Secondly, we must just not be reaching them effectively. Now the question became:* "What can I do to open the floodgates of qualified potential employees coming into my stores and putting in their applications?"
>
> *That was a qualitatively different question that was spurred only the negative question of* "Should we lower our standards?" *It was a challenging question that allowed me to dig deeper.*
>
> *After asking the question, I got quiet. I didn't try to answer the question immediately. I stood up from*

my chair and grabbed my cell phone and called my marketing rep.

At the time, we had a monthly contract for radio advertising for our regular business. I asked my marketing rep if it would be a problem for us to change the radio ad for a few weeks. What would the process be to change from product advertising, to advertising our need for good quality employees for our stores? I wanted to know if we could change out for a few weeks, and then return to product advertising at a later date.

The answers I received back were that it was possible and workable, and that it would probably be effective. Now instead of going online or putting ads in the newspaper looking for employees, the message would go out to a few hundred thousand citizens living in this particular area—many of whom were surely looking for employment. It worked and the problem was solved.

The idea came from contemplating for a few minutes in a quiet space. It was based on the determination of my mission—that of attracting qualified people to come and work for me.

The outcome might have been different had I agreed with the question: "Should we lower our standards?" *We could have closed the floodgates of people who wanted to come to work for us.*

I did not know the answer to this dilemma going in. In fact, I had spent almost a half hour listening to how bad the problem was. But by maintaining my inspiration and asking the right questions, creativity was released and the answer came.

Suspend Negativity

If you're asking a person a question, think of how you might contribute their best, most confident attributes. Think of how you can help that person take the next step to go towards that goal.

Basically, you suspend any negativity you may be feeling. In the story of Sol and the operations manager, he did not belittle her for voicing a negative question. He moved past her question to access the infinite resources within himself to get things done.

Ask a question, engaging infinite resources that are available to you that you may have never engaged before. Structure the question in such a way that it empowers you (or the person you are asking) to use your best talents, skills and resources. You ask it is such a way that you are able to take action. You feel great and you help other people to feel powerful.

And it may not even be that you "feel great" but at least you know you can take action. You can take the next step and resolve whatever problem you are facing, because you have that power.

Right after you ask the question, take a moment of silence to engage your creativity. It is important that you focus on the outcome, imagining what the outcome will feel like. Engage your creativity which is in the space from which unexpected ideas come.

You are Always Creative

The sad thing is that often people do more to hamper their creativity than need to evoke it. One must learn to postulate the notion that *you are always creative!* You may not be aware of it, but you are always in the process of bringing something new to life. Literally, you are doing it with your breath. You are breathing in new air every time you take a breath. You are constantly creating new blood cells.

That goes back to the point that after you have asked a question, stop and breathe. By stopping for a moment, you will not overpower what could come next with your own momentum of thought. It's not so much what you *have* to do to access creativity, its more about simply getting quiet and letting the genius inside you spring forth.

* * *

As the two men were getting ready to leave the restaurant, Ron commented that he was eager to learn more about asking the "right" questions. To which Sol replied, "It's not so much a matter of being right or wrong. Rather, there are questions which may be more empowering—or more effective—in a certain situation or circumstance. That's the key to discovering high-quality questions."

"I hear you." Ron grabbed the check just as Sol was reaching for it. "Then I'll look for more opportunities to ask *empowering* questions. Ones that will trigger and release creativity!"

Chapter 6

Empowerment

Implementing the Principles

"Can I get you another piece of pie?" offered Ron's wife, Gina. She waved toward the deep dish apple pie in the center of the table where two pieces remained.

Sol shook his head. "Thank you, but I don't think I could eat another bite. Everything was delicious. But I would take a refill on the coffee."

As Gina filled his cup, Sol said, "Ron's been bragging to me about your cooking. But now I see he had every reason to brag. Best lasagna I've eaten in a long time."

Gina smiled at her husband. "He knows how to make points," she teased.

"So now," Ron put in, "when Gina asked you if you wanted more pie, that was a non-creative, disempowering, low-quality question leading only to a yes or no answer." Then he laughed at his own joke. "Tell us Sol, how could that have been a more empowering question?"

"That's easy," Sol said lifting his coffee mug as if in a salute. "She could have asked, 'What could I do to make it possible for you to enjoy more pie?' I then would have tapped into my creativity, thinking for a moment, then I would have answered, 'Put a piece of pie in a to-go box!'"

Laughter sounded around the table as they all enjoyed the joke.

Gina caught on quickly because Ron had been explaining to her the concepts of asking high-quality questions. In fact, the two of them had been working at implementing the principles in their conversations with one another.

Facing Negative Attitudes

A few weeks earlier, Ron had mentioned to his new friend that he wanted Sol to meet Gina. Finally, the opportunity had presented itself where there was a free evening and Michael was staying overnight with a friend.

After the table was cleared and the trio had retreated to the couches in the den, Ron brought up the subject of negativity. "Even though I'm learning many of the concepts that we've been discussing, I am still a little confused when faced with a roomful of negative attitudes.

"It might be in a sales meeting or it might be in staff meeting with other department heads in the company. During those sessions, I pretty much feel disempowered."

Your Ability to Create Value

Earlier in the evening Sol had been discussing the subject of empowerment and how important it is in the question-asking process. But Ron didn't see how it could work in the heavy atmosphere of negative ideas, opinions and attitudes. He had to admit his reaction was usually that of anger and frustration and told Sol as much.

"One of the things that I have learned in my experience," Sol told him as he settled back on the couch, "is that all situations can be used in service of your purpose. Therefore, I look at negativity as being useful.

"Question quality can be measured in the amount of confidence standing behind it. Remember we talked about the fact that one of the biggest contributors to negativity is fear."

Ron nodded. "I remember talking about that. I also remember that you said that 'confidence is the capability to transform fear into very specific thinking and action using your best skills with your best resources.'"

"Precisely. That means that when you are faced with a great deal of fear being generated through a great deal of negativity, then *you* have the ability to create value by simply using *your* confidence to transform it."

Ron was shaking his head. He wasn't too sure about that. "That sounds like a pretty tall order to me."

"But it's not really. In fact, once you begin to take it apart and study it, it's quite simple."

* * *

What do You Want to Accomplish?

In a negative situation, stop and think: What do you actually want to accomplish? Get a very clear intention—a very clear goal. After you know when your timed goal is actually going to take place, and what you are actually going to be achieving, negativity becomes very useful. The way you focus negativity is to very discretely separate out all the objections that are raised against the idea being presented.

The goal here is to divide and conquer those obstacles by coming up with a quality question to each of them. The negativity then becomes useful in the question-asking process. You can channel it by deciding exactly what it is that is stopping you from getting to what you determine you actually want. And then, you ask, "*How can we resolve just this one obstacle?*"

When someone is bringing up negative points saying such and so can never be done, or there's not enough money in the budget, or corporate would never go for that—those negative statements present the opportunity for empowering questions to come forth. For example: "What can we do in the next week (or month or six months) to make this happen?"

Obstacles Become Stepping Stones

The obstacles—the negative thinking—become stepping stones to creative thinking that empowers others to take action. By simply asking questions about each of the obstacles, asking how they can be conquered, can work to bring ideas and creativity into the picture.

The negative people in your life have a place. If you can learn to metabolize them effectively, they can help you get what you want—more so even than the friends who are agreeing with you and patting you on the back.

If everything were easy and we had no level of resistance in our lives, we would never have the ability to grow. It's how we use that resistance that decides whether we get trapped or set free.

When you come into a time of opposition or negativity—obstacles lie in your path. It may be those who disagree with, or negate, your ideas and plans. Or it may be someone who is upset with you, be it a customer, a subordinate, a peer, or a superior.

Creativity Springs Forth

It was discussed in an earlier chapter about the source of value. Does your source of value come from within you? Or does it come from being right in a certain situation? (In other words, being in control). Because, now you are faced with a choice. You must decide what you will ask in order to take you in a specific direction. What will transform the negative into empowerment?

Most people aren't aware enough to realize that what they do next will either expand the current negative situation (obstacles) or it will allow creativity to spring forth in a way that they will be able to take this current obstacle and turn it to where they wanted it to go.

Obstacles can become an opportunity to communicate and get creative. It's an opportunity to engage the obstacles at their best and highest purposes. When someone brings you an obstacle, you get to engage them; you get to have a moment of creativity. Once you grasp this concept, you will look at the world differently. Rather than allow anger and frustration to arise, you choose to move into a state of creativity.

Honor and Value the Person

Facing the problem you ask yourself: *What do I really want to create today?* And then you ask: *What am I after right now?* Then you recall your basic intention. Take a second and breathe. Consider the fact that there is value right here in the world that you are creating. Remember that the person (or persons) in front of you is a glorious human being, worthy of respect simply because he or she is a creation of the natural universe.

Let's say someone has made a glaring error and messed everything up. You can either ask: "This thing is a mess. What were you thinking?" or you can say: "Peter, this is all wrong. But I know you have the potential to do much better. What are some of the things we can work on, and how can we get the needed help to get this project done by nine o'clock tomorrow morning? What needs to happen between now and nine o'clock in the morning for us to get this project done and out of here?"

Because high-quality questions have been asked, empowerment has been released into the situation for all concerned. Action steps will be taken.

There are those who will protest that you must assess the problem before you can get things done, or get it resolved. That's true—there is a time for process development and improvement of communication. However, if you are in a situation where time and resources are limited, concentrating on the cause of the problem is not the route to take at the moment. If you have to choose between getting the results you're after or spending time analyzing the results that you didn't get, guess which one is a better use of your time and resources? The former, of course.

Example of Transferring Negative to Empowerment

As the evening's conversation between Sol and Ron continued, Sol gave a vivid example of from transferring the negative over to empowerment.

> *I was once engaged in a business that was growing, but it wasn't growing fast enough. Basically, I didn't have much confidence in the managers. Upon further investigation, I learned that these managers were stealing from me. I learned that they had stolen a significant amount of money and that they were going to leave very soon. I remember that I looked at the finances of the business and saw that we were bleeding to the tune of between fifty to sixty thousand dollars per month.*
>
> *This was an extremely difficult time. I contacted a private investor and I said that we needed need a cash injection or the business was going to collapse. I was extended $40,000, but they said,* "After this, there is no more. I can't extend any more to you."
>
> *I remember going home that day and thinking about the implication of losing fifty grand a month and only having forty thousand left. That amounted to less than one month's operating capital.*
>
> *This happened in the middle of the summer, and at that time we had already been struggling for quite a while. As I pondered the problem I made a profound statement:* "I am going to get this business through this time."
>
> *Following the statement I asked this question:* "What action can I take in the next twenty four to forty eight hours that would allow my business to break even in one hundred and twenty days or less?"
>
> *Now it was no longer about the fifty thousand dollar problem. I wasn't even focused there. Nor did I expend any wasted energy in anger or frustration toward these*

managers. I was focused on what I could do in the next hour, and in the hour after that, and then in the next day to move this business from losing fifty thousand dollars a month to losing nothing in four months or less.

Right after I asked the question I got very quiet. It was as if I were focusing on the outcome. I knew at that moment it was important to not focus on the problem (the negative). I knew that if I focused on the problem, the problem would expand. If I focused on the solution, it would open the door to incredible empowerment.

From that moment on we took action. We did all kinds of things. It wasn't just me; it was about mobilizing my entire staff to get it done.

We maintained our staffing at a different level. We made numerous phone calls. We visited other businesses and suggested our services. We focused on customers who had come to us in the past. We polled our staff for ideas. The next forty-eight hours were a blur. I don't even remember all of the things that happened. I just remember being intent on taking serious action, based on a limited time frame and a specific outcome.

Rather than wringing my hands and lamenting about the negative circumstances, I asked questions that were specifically focused on the desired outcome.

Along the way to reaching our goal we re-designed our systems to make it impossible for anyone to steal in the same way again. In that respect, I was thankful for the theft as I became aware of the vulnerability of the old system.

Additionally, we set about to incentivize future managers, so it was more advantageous for them to engage us than steal from us

In that area the question I asked was, "How do we engage people to be as honest and as creative as they can be with us and give us the best of their efforts?" *We had to get make sure that we didn't shut ourselves down by bringing negative intentions into our activity.*

In this situation, it was not a matter of positive or negative so much as it was the efficiency of the outcome. Our outcome was well defined and we were empowered to move toward our goals with a great degree of creativity. In the final analysis that goal was reached.

* * *

By the time Sol left Ron's house that evening, the younger man had an entirely new perspective on how to handle negative circumstances. Now instead of dreading such times, he looked forward to them as moments in which he could empower and create!

Chapter 7

Moving Forward

Questions that Lead to Positive Actions

The stores lining the boulevard across from the park were bright with Christmas decorations. Sol sat on his favorite park bench watching Ron teach Michael how to skip stones on the surface of the lake. The rookie had changed perceptively, both in his actions and in his thinking, since the two first met.

Presently, Ron strolled over and sat down by Sol. "Look at that!" Sol pointed to where Michael had just executed three full skips with a rock. "I think he's getting the hang of it." He slapped Ron on the shoulder. "You're a good teacher."

"I guess it's no secret that our Saturdays are a lot different than they used to be."

"And why is that?"

"First of all I stopped asking Michael dead-end questions. Or as you would call them, disempowering questions."

Sol chuckled. "Good work. Then what?"

"One night when I was tucking him in for the night, I asked, 'Michael, what can we do to make our Saturdays together better?'" Ron shook his head. "That's when I learned that he had absolutely no interest in playing soccer. Surprise! The rest of the items on his list were such things as slow down, talk more, and enjoy the park."

"Hmm. Enjoy the park. Like catching toads and skipping rocks?"

"Exactly. Then we looked at the list to see what was workable. Since there was only one more game in the soccer season, that was simple. After that we began to implement his plan."

"And you're pleased with the results?" Sol asked, still watching Michael at play.

"More than pleased. I'm thrilled. And so is Gina. Now before I ask Michael a question, I stop and ask myself, 'What can he do next?' After the question is asked will it lead to confusion and disempowerment? Or will it lead to positive action?"

"A good test for the quality of any question."

Ron laughed. "I only learn from the best."

* * *

What Do You Do Next?

When presenting a question—even to yourself in self talk—the best qualifier for the question is "What do you do next?" If you ask a question and it creates a sense of disempowerment, or confusion, or procrastination, that will lend a clue to the inspiration or the intention behind the question.

What do you do next? How do you feel about your next action? Do you feel confident that you can make some kind of change? Confident that you can make some kind of move or some kind of positive action? If so, then you know that that is a high-quality question and is beneficial to your cause.

If what results is confusion, dissonance, or a lack of focus, it may direct your attention that you are not asking optimal questions. Once you begin to understand and appreciate what happens in your body and your mind after you've asked a question, then you can begin to work on asking questions that are of a higher quality.

One of the things to consider with respect to the question quality is something called a *range of possibility*.

The range of possibility can be described as a particular *feeling*. You may feel like you can take very confident steps or you may feel like you need to sit and wait for a while. You need to meditate longer on whatever the answer is. Either way is fine. What you must beware of is the quality of that action right after you ask a question.

Oftentimes questions are asked with a range of *expectations* for where the answer will fall. You have to be careful about where your "self positions" lie as you ask a specific type of question.

Someone might ask something as simple as "Why are you such a moron?"

This is asked with a range of *expectation,* or preconditioned, predetermined, limited ideas. In other words, the one asking has a pre-determined answer in mind, such as: "You just are, that's all. You can't help it."

The range of *possibilities* for actions after such a question is posed is extremely limited. You either have, *Yes, I am a moron,* and what do you do next with that? Not much.

Or the answer is *No, I am not a moron.* Now you've created a defensive disposition which sets the scene for a confrontational exchange. For the person who is already angry about something, this is a great way to fuel a heated exchange and allow steam to blow off. But the range of possibility for that question is short, and basically non-productive.

Opportunities to use this application are infinite. The *range of possibilities* concept can be used in how one communicates with self and with other people.

Confidence Levels

As you examine the intentions behind the question, you will soon discover that the measure of question quality is ***how the range of possibility interacts with your level of confidence.***

We can conclude then that question quality is a function of your range of possibilities *and* the function of your confidence. If your question makes you (or the person to whom you are posing the question) feel more confident and with a bigger range of possibility than before the question was asked, then that was a beneficial question. Whereas, if you have the opposite effect, then you realize you are asking disempowering questions which will lead to disempowering results.

Because the range of possibilities is strongly connected with a person's level of confidence, it stands to reason that a person with a low level of self confidence (one with low self esteem, or little belief in self) will tend to ask disempowering, non-productive questions. They are questions that reaffirm a pre-supposed belief, or will serve to make that person *feel that he or she is right.* The need to feel right comes ahead of the desire for productive solutions.

For instance, Ron's fear of his subordinates drove him to ask demanding, investigative questions that left little room for a wide range of possibilities. "Why didn't that get done?" "Why are your quotas down?" "Why were you late?"

Knowing why you didn't do something doesn't empower that activity to get done. In fact, such questions cut off the ability to "take action steps" toward good solutions.

Also due to Ron's lack of confidence in this area, he succeeded only in getting the results that he felt he deserved (whether consciously or subconsciously). The atmosphere in the sales room was often electric with defensive attitudes and a degree of belligerence. Which was what he had expected.

In addition, Ron had the notion that being *nice* was a show of weakness. Sol pointed out that it wasn't about sugar coating, or being nice. It has to do with being respectful. It has to do with honoring the other person's capacity to bring value. You have to honor your own capacity to bring value and you have to be willing to work with people.

Ron quickly saw that he hadn't been trained to think efficiently about managing his intentions with the questions he asked. When he began to use high-quality, empowering questions aimed at group solutions, the atmosphere—which was more relaxed—became charged with ideas and a wide range of possibilities.

This goes back to the state you are in when you ask a question. The fact is, each person possesses *enough* within themselves to ask great questions. The range of possibilities is completely dependent on the person who is contending behind it.

When asking self-questions, ninety-nine percent of the time people can answer their own questions. They know the answers. And if they do that enough (practice and train), very soon a sense of self sufficiency will kick in.

Taking Action

Sol taught his new prodigy the importance of how to step into action following an empowering question. In order to take action, relax for a time and focus intently on the outcome. Pause to see what your naturally, incredible, creative mind throws at you next. *Then move in that direction.*

Hesitation and procrastination at this point can be lethal to the outcome. It's at this very moment that we are most susceptible to fear; it's where fear can do the most damage. We can command our creativity to start working for us after asking an empowering question, but then we run the risk of allowing fear to stop us from moving.

When the creativity begins, you may be thrown an answer from your mind, but you feel the need to stop and analyze it, rather than taking the step to make it happen.

What's so great about taking action is that even if you are wrong—even if you are totally wrong—if you remain open, chances are you will learn from that wrong action and you will learn quickly. Meanwhile, momentum has started and that action will usually lead to another, and another. As the momentum builds, more and more options will become available to you as you continue to work on your problem.

Control

You can spend an eternity trying to figuring out what's wrong—what's wrong with you; what's wrong with the system; what's wrong with your plan; what's wrong with your employees, what's wrong with your business plan, and on and on. While you may or may not discover "what's wrong" realize that nothing will ever be perfect. Rather than focus on what's wrong, work toward something that *will work*. Move towards something that will produce the energy, money, and resources to make things better.

A wonderful quote from the world-famous inventor Thomas A. Edison demonstrates the point more clearly:

> ***Results? Why, man, I have gotten lots of results! If I find 10,000 ways something won't work, I haven't failed. I am not discouraged, because every wrong attempt discarded is often a step forward*** . . . .

Seeing the Impossible as Possible

The opportunity for us to make progress begins with our belief that the seemingly impossible is possible. We must remain loyal to our commitment to bring forth our highest and best plans and projections; we ask questions to view reality appropriately. In other words, to understand that which we can and cannot control.

The need to control is often based on the belief of a lack of resources—which is rooted in fear. Ron believed that he lacked the support of his subordinates and as a result, he was fearful. When, in fact, he was at all times surrounded by more than enough resources to make their sales team a top-ranking team.

Sol helped him to see that each person can only control two things in their world: How you interpret and how you respond. You control how you interpret information and how you act based on that information. That's it. You have nothing else.

You don't control how people act. You don't control what things costs. You don't control how your body functions. You don't control what people say. You don't control how people interpret things.

All you control are those two things. How information flows in and out of your body. When you are working with those two things, you realize that your perspective is a part of that control volume—part of that control mechanism. That perspective, then, equips you with the ability to ask high-quality, empowering questions.

As you become really good at focusing on those two areas, you can let all the rest of it happen. You recognize that your life will continue whether or not you get this thing that you think is really important. And your need for control of other things diminishes greatly. Stress is reduced and quality of life expands.

Summing Up

Many times we simply go through the motions of living life. We admire and pay high respect to professional athletes who are at the top of their form. We recognize that they spend hours in diligent physical and mental workouts.

On the other hand, we have the capability and the potential to practice quality living every day. Yet, we don't train like we're actually playing a really important game.

One can train to perfect the level of intention, by simply knowing and being alert to what you want to achieve in any conversation with yourself or with others. Become aware of what it is you actually want in this world in order to thrive.

If you have an interaction with a co-worker, and they bring forth a very negative statement or ask a negative question, train yourself to step back and think for a moment.

"What is my objective with respect to this person?"

"What do I really want?"

"What is the best situation?"

"What is the best possible manifestation of life with this person in this moment?"

"What can I actually achieve through this interaction?"

With this approach (which requires training and practice) you basically give the best of yourself to every person and every thought in your world. You are being alert to bring your best effort and your best intention to every moment. In time, you will engage and regard your highest and best intention at every point in every day.

The truth is, you don't even need to look that far ahead. Do it right this very moment and see what happens.

ROBERT SHEMIN

Internationally-respected Wealth Creation Expert and current *New York Times'* bestselling author Robert Shemin first became a millionaire at the age of just 32. But he didn't want to keep all of his wealth-building strategies and financial know-how to himself. He's taught tens of thousands of Americans the secrets to attracting, growing, and securing lasting wealth through his best-selling books and countless sold-out seminars held to standing-room-only crowds in cities across the United States.

Once considered "least likely to succeed," Shemin overcame severe learning disabilities and seemingly insurmountable odds to become one of the most charismatic and sought after lecturers and motivational speakers in the country, helping thousands of hardworking Americans of all different backgrounds attain total financial freedom for life even though most of his protégés had no investment experience, no financial savvy, and zero money in the bank.

Regularly sharing the podium with such financial luminaries as Donald Trump, Robert Kiyosaki, David Bach, Suze Orman and Tony Robbins, Shemin helped create The Learning Annex Wealth Expo and has consistently been voted the "#1 speaker" by crowds of over 50,000 people.

Robert Shemin has worked with high-net-worth individuals from Goldman Sachs, helped create four companies, and, as a full-time investor, been involved in over 1,000 real-estate transactions to date totaling nearly 100 million dollars.

He is the author of ten bestselling books including, *Secrets of A Millionaire Real Estate Investor, Successful Real Estate Investing—How to Avoid the 75 Most Costly Mistakes Every Investor Makes, Secrets of Buying and Selling Real Estate—Without Using Your Own Money, Secrets of a Millionaire Landlord, Unlimited Riches, 40 Days to Success in Real Estate Investing*, and his newest release, *How Come that Idiot's Rich and I'm Not?*, a current *Wall Street Journal* and *New York Times'* bestseller.

Shemin serves on the faculty of The Mentor Financial Group; enjoys the endorsement of The Mr. Landlord Organization; and is a spokesperson for The National Association of Real Estate Investors and the American Congress of Real Estate Investors.

Robert's Shemin Wealth Academy conducts events with a unique delivery of his knowledge and a powerful masterful authority of his work, time and again he receives high accolades from his audiences as one of the most dynamic and compelling speakers of our time. Robert shares all of his secrets for success at these events.

An expert on wealth for CNN, Robert Shemin is a frequent guest on national, regional, and local television and radio programs such as National Public Radio (NPR) and CNBC's "The Big Idea" with Donny Deutsch. He has also been featured in over three hundred newspapers and magazines including *BusinessWeek,* the *Los Angeles Times,* the *Miami Herald,* the *New York Post, USA Today, the Wall Street Journal, and TIME Magazine among many others.*

With a heart as big as his bank account, Shemin gives generously to numerous charitable endeavors such as the homeless, those in need of critical eye operations overseas, and at-risk teens and college-age youth in Israel through the formation of a specialized school he founded and successfully operates. As experienced as Shemin is at showing high-net-worth individuals how to get richer, his real love however is helping self-described "financial disasters" earn millions.

Robert Shemin holds a law degree and an MBA from Emory University.

For additional information about Robert Shemin and a list of his many topics to fit the need of your event, please contact him at 888-302-8018.

HUGH STEWART

Hugh Stewart's education is both diverse and substantial. He has two degrees from the University of Miami; an undergraduate and a graduate degree in Mechanical Engineering. He is also a graduate of the Strategic Coach® program and is currently enrolled in the Strategic Coach® Masters Program.

Hugh currently serves as a Major in the United States Air Force Auxiliary with a specialization in cadet programs. Between 1995-2009, he was responsible for training five nationally recognized cadet competition teams.

Hugh has a diverse and successful business background; not only is he a Nuclear Fuel Designer, but he has created and operated over seventeen businesses in the past 10 years in industries such as money services, real estate, advertising, insurance consulting, and coaching.

Business partnerships are an important aspect to the success of many and Hugh is no exception. He has been involved in over nine partnerships. In these partnerships, he has functioned in the various roles of employee, independent contractor, strategic partner, joint venture partner and equity partner, in various types of corporate structures including LLCs, corporations, and non-profit organizations. With his practical understanding of what makes and breaks a partnership, he is uniquely capable to give guidance on creating, maintaining, and planning for the dissolution of these relationships.

With a practical understanding of creating, operating, and maintaining a business as an entrepreneur and as a business partner, Hugh has acquired the experience and knowledge of what it takes to be successful in business. This knowledge is what he shares with his coaching clients.

One of Hugh's strongest influences was at the age of twenty, when he received some invaluable advice and a copy of a book that started his life in a new direction. The book was *Rich Dad, Poor Dad*, by Robert Kiyosaki. It was the first book he ever read on wealth and wealth creation and made a huge impact on the direction of his life.

Hugh was fascinated in how coaches are able to empower people's thinking, foster incredible communication and create extraordinary value. He realized he had this ability to convey and consult and began his journey to inspire and empower others on how to achieve goals.

For additional information about Hugh Stewart and a list of his many topics to fit the need of your event, please contact him through his website located at www.confidentsolutionscoach.com.

www.ingramcontent.com/pod-product-compliance
Lightning Source LLC
Chambersburg PA
CBHW021914170526
45157CB00005B/2065
* 9 7 8 1 4 6 2 0 2 8 3 1 3 *